**THIS BOOK
BELONGS TO:**

"HE'S NOT WORTH IT!"

OF ALL THE POST-BREAKUP CLICHÉS THAT GET THROWN AT YOU, THIS IS THE ONE THAT ROLLS OFF THE TONGUE THE FASTEST. YOU MIGHT EVEN THINK THE FRIENDS WHO PREACH IT ARE JUST BEING LAZY WITH THEIR ADVICE. BUT GUESS WHAT? IT'S COMPLETELY FUCKING TRUE.

HE'S NOT WORTH IT

A Journal For Ending
the Toxic Cycle,
Taking Control of
Your Emotions, and
Finding True Love

JULIE DAY

CASTLE POINT BOOKS
NEW YORK

www.castlepointbooks.com

The Castle Point Books trademark is owned by Castle Point Publishing, LLC.
Castle Point books are published and distributed by St. Martin's Publishing Group.

ISBN 978-1-250-28209-5 (trade paperback)

Cover and interior design by Melissa Gerber
Composition by Noora Cox
Editorial by Monica Sweeney
Images used under license by Shutterstock.com

Our books may be purchased in bulk for promotional, educational, or business
use. Please contact your local bookseller or the Macmillan Corporate and
Premium Sales Department at 1-800-221-7945, extension 5442, or by email at
MacmillanSpecialMarkets@macmillan.com.

First Edition: 2023

10 9 8 7 6 5 4 3 2 1

Nothing compares to a broken heart, or to the feelings of panic when some reminder of what once was rains down from the sky to throw you off balance. These feelings of sadness, frustration, and even embarrassment can be relentless and exhausting, but just like You-Know-Who plaguing your thoughts, they are rentals.

He's Not Worth It is more than just a place to vent your feelings. It's like the friend who's shaking you awake to your own magnificence. It's here to help bring you closer to the long-term contentment of knowing your worth and knowing how to choose the relationships that feel like home.

No matter how you handle a shattered heart—by picking up the pieces quietly by yourself or by trying to fashion a weapon out of the tiny shards that are left—there comes a time when you have to find the glue so you can keep going.

So, take those pieces and make a kaleidoscope to see all the gorgeous possibilities in front of you. Because the one who's worth it is you.

IF YOU DON'T
SETTLE FOR
ALL THESE IDIOTS
OUT THERE, THE
GOOD ONE IS
GOING TO COME.....
WHEN YOU SET
THE STANDARD
FOR YOURSELF,
THE TIDE RISES.

— Chelsea Handler, The Daily Show

No, Queen

Your life is your kingdom, and who you invite to bow at your throne better be worthy.

What new standards are you ready to set for yourself?

_____

_____

_____

_____

What didn't you expect from a partner before that you now know you deserve?

_____

_____

_____

A RELATIONSHIP,
I THINK, IS LIKE A SHARK.
YOU KNOW? IT HAS
TO CONSTANTLY MOVE
FORWARD OR IT DIES.
AND I THINK WHAT WE
GOT ON OUR HANDS
IS A DEAD SHARK.

— Alvy Singer, Annie Hall

Dead in the Water

It's hard to watch a relationship die, but it's even worse to be in a relationship that is *very dead* while one or both parties desperately tries to poke it, prod it, coo at it, and act like there might be a miraculous resurrection. What fears do you have in letting go and moving on?

_____

_____

_____

_____

_____

_____

_____

_____

NEVER DULL YOUR SHINE FOR SOMEBODY ELSE.

— Tyra Banks

Shine
Bright, Babe

And why exactly is it your problem if he can't deal with your brilliance? Think of a time when you dimmed your light to make a guy feel more comfortable or because he made you feel bad. What would it feel like if you decided to blind him with all that light instead?

_____

_____

_____

_____

_____

_____

_____

_____

_____

I HAD TO PAY
FOR ALL OF YOUR
BAD BEHAVIOR, BUT
EXPENSIVE LESSONS
ARE ALWAYS THE
BEST TO KNOW.

— Elle King, "The Let Go"

Right On the Money

Emotional sticker shock is real. When you are constantly tabulating the consequences of someone's behavior, you start to wonder if the expense is really worth it. What lessons have cost you the most?

_____

_____

_____

_____

_____

_____

_____

_____

_____

_____

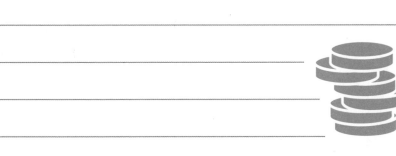

NOT EVERYONE
THAT'S HURT
YOU CARES.
FORGIVENESS
LETS YOU OFF
THE HOOK.

— Sandra Bullock,
The Kelly Clarkson Show

He Just Doesn't Give AF

Does this person care that they hurt you? If yes, roll again.
If no: Why are you playing this game?! Here is your *Get Out of Your Own Emotional Jail Free* card. The longer you wait for apologies or better conduct, the more emotional exhaustion you'll face with nothing to show for it. Imagine a world in which you're not burdened by this and instead you're living your life. What would feel good to be able to forgive, if only for yourself?

_____

_____

_____

_____

_____

_____

YOU SEEM TO MATCH YOUR SELF-ESTEEM WITH YOUR PARTNER.

— Dax Shepherd, Armchair Expert

Mirror, Mirror

Take a look at your past partners : The nice one! The toxic one! The one who never got off the couch!

What does this person say about how you felt about yourself at the time?

_____

_____

_____

What characteristics in a partner would positively reflect the healthiest parts of yourself?

_____

_____

_____

_____

TAKE YOUR BROKEN HEART, MAKE IT INTO ART.

— Carrie Fisher

Heart Full

Broken shards can cut, or they can become a thing of beauty. In the heart below, name the feelings that feel most intense right now. Outside the shape, list the feelings you miss having and that you know will someday return. Use colors and doodles to fill in the spaces.

THE TIME YOU SPEND HATING ON SOMEONE ROBS YOU OF YOUR OWN TIME. YOU ARE LITERALLY HATING ON YOURSELF AND YOU DON'T EVEN REALIZE IT.

— Joe Rogan, Joe Rogan: Podcasts, Pot, and Persistence

How Do I Hate Thee?

Let me count the ways! Turns out spending all your waking moments wrapped up in hatred is a real time suck. In what ways have you exhausted your own personal time digging into your negative emotions? How could you utilize that time differently?

_____

_____

_____

_____

_____

_____

_____

_____

_____

_____

YOU KNOW,
IT'S FUNNY.
WHEN YOU LOOK AT
SOMEONE THROUGH
ROSE-COLORED GLASSES,
ALL THE RED FLAGS
JUST LOOK LIKE FLAGS.

— Wanda Pierce, Bojack Horseman

Love is Blind

Sort of! Sometimes those neon signs to stay away are *very* obvious.

Make a list of the red flags you have ignored in the past.

1. _____

2. _____

3. _____

4. _____

Make a list of the green flags you should look for in the future.

1. _____

2. _____

3. _____

4. _____

YOU'RE A GOOD PERSON— UNDERNEATH ALL YOUR BAD QUALITIES.

— Nico, *The Sex Lives of College Girls*

Mr. Right
and Wrong

Some people are assholes, end of story. Other people are good (okay, *mediocre*) and, under pressure or in the wrong relationship, make choices befitting an asshole. What are the redeeming qualities of the people you have dated? If they don't have any, write "I will never date an asshole again" as many times as you can fit below.

_____

_____

_____

_____

_____

_____

_____

_____

WHEN SOMEONE SHOWS YOU THEIR TRUE COLORS, BELIEVE THEM!

— Dolly Parton

Color
the Truth

Adult coloring, you say? How fun! When has someone shown you their true colors? If you were to give these characteristics or events actual color, what images come to mind? Draw them here.

I HAD ABSOLUTELY NO INTEREST IN BEING SOMEBODY ELSE'S MUSE. I AM NOT A MUSE. I AM THE SOMEBODY. END OF FUCKING STORY.

— Taylor Jenkins Reid, Daisy Jones & The Six

Your Magnum Opus

Don't let someone else's vision cloud yours. When has someone tried to treat you like their pet project? What are you capable of that they underestimated?

_____

_____

_____

_____

_____

_____

_____

_____

THE POOR WISH
TO BE RICH,
THE RICH WISH
TO BE HAPPY,
THE SINGLE WISH
TO BE MARRIED,
AND THE MARRIED
WISH TO BE DEAD.

— *Ann Landers*

The Grass Is Always Greener...

When it's watered by an actual professional. Take time to admire what's already in your garden. What do you envy about other people's dating lives? What could you spend more time cultivating and nurturing in your own?

_____

_____

_____

_____

_____

_____

_____

_____

EVERY PERSON ON
THIS EARTH NEEDS
JUST ONE PERSON
WHO SEES THEM AND
ROOTS FOR THEM.
DEEPLY, TRULY.
ONE PERSON.
IT'S WHAT WE ALL
NEED TO GET THROUGH.
THE MORE THE MERRIER
BUT LET'S START
WITH ONE.

— Selma Blair, Mean Baby

#1

Rooting for You!

There's always that someone in the background, listening to your highs and lows, cheering you on with a "get it, girl" and a "he's dead to me" at all the right moments. Who is this person for you? When did you most appreciate their rah-rah attitude?

_____

_____

_____

_____

_____

_____

_____

_____

_____

REBECCA WELTON:
NOW WE'RE IN
A BIT OF A
LIMBO SITUATION.

TED LASSO:
GREAT PARTY GAME,
HORRIBLE
RELATIONSHIP STATUS.

— Ted Lasso

How Low Can You Go?

When it comes to limbo, someone always ends up a winner, and another person ends up on their ass. When have you felt relationship limbo? What or who was the reason for getting out of it?

_____

_____

_____

_____

_____

_____

_____

_____

_____

WE HAVE TO BE WHOLE PEOPLE TO FIND WHOLE LOVE, EVEN IF WE HAVE TO MAKE IT UP FOR A WHILE.

— Cheryl Strayed, Dear Sugar

The Whole Package

You can't get anywhere on an empty tank, and you can't be fully invested in a relationship if you haven't invested in yourself.

When has treating yourself with more love benefited those around you?

_____

_____

_____

If you invest in yourself now, what parts of you need the most attention?

_____

_____

_____

I NEVER HATED A MAN ENOUGH TO GIVE HIS DIAMONDS BACK.

— Zsa Zsa Gabor

Parting Gifts

Take the gems of a relationship with you when you go. Some are giant, blinding rocks; others require a very powerful magnifying loupe to see the sparkle. But the sparkles—those memories worth savoring or the moments that act as lessons—are yours to keep. What do you hold fondness for in a past relationship?

_____

_____

_____

_____

_____

_____

_____

_____

_____

IF YOU DON'T LOVE YOURSELF, HOW IN THE HELL YOU GONNA LOVE SOMEBODY ELSE?

— RuPaul

Love You, Mean It

Take the energy you'd put into a relationship and put it into a relationship with yourself. How do you need to be wooed?

_____

_____

_____

_____

_____

_____

_____

_____

_____

_____

_____

I THINK YOU'RE
JUST REMEMBERING
THE GOOD STUFF.
NEXT TIME YOU
LOOK BACK, I, UH,
I REALLY THINK YOU
SHOULD LOOK AGAIN.

— Rachel Hansen,
500 Days of Summer

Double Vision

It's important to remember the good, but not if it means you're ignoring the bad. When have you sugar-coated a relationship or a situation—and why?

_____

_____

_____

_____

_____

_____

_____

_____

_____

_____

WE ARE NEVER EVER, EVER GETTING BACK TOGETHER.

— Taylor Swift,
"We Are Never Ever Getting Back Together"

Like, Ever

It's not a breakup if you don't stick the landing. When have you been wishy-washy about a breakup? What has felt or would feel good about a clean break?

_____

_____

_____

_____

_____

_____

_____

_____

_____

_____

_____

IF YOU'RE LOOKING FOR SYMPATHY YOU CAN FIND IT BETWEEN SHIT AND SYPHILIS IN THE DICTIONARY.

— David Sedaris, Barrel Fever

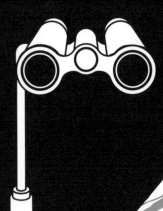

Best Wishes/ Warmest Regards

Funny thing about sympathy: everyone has a limit. Maybe this is because you've *exhaustively* talked a friend's ear off and you refuse to take their advice. Or maybe you need a confidant, but your go-to just isn't in the right headspace to be supportive. The good news is—you can always be your own best friend! What do you most need to hear right now?

_____

_____

_____

_____

_____

_____

YOU DON'T HAVE TO BE SORRY FOR DOING IT ON YOUR OWN.

— Harry Styles, "Matilda"

Flying Solo

No sorries here. What's the best part of being no-strings-attached?

_____

_____

_____

_____

_____

_____

_____

_____

_____

_____

_____

_____

MOLLY CARTER:
YOU GOTTA FUCK
A LOT OF FROGS TO
GET A GOOD FROG.

ISSA DEE:
THAT'S NOT THE SAYING.
OR ANY SAYING.

— *Insecure*

Prince Charming-ish

Is your list of frogs long or short? What's your funniest or most memorable frog story?

_____

_____

_____

_____

_____

_____

_____

_____

_____

_____

LIFE IS UNFAIR, AND SOMETIMES IT HELPS TO **IRRATIONALLY BLAME** SOMEONE FOR IT.

— *Michelle Zauner, Crying in H Mart*

Hello, My Name is Petty Bitch

It's like that sometimes, when you just need to vent, to commiserate, to take the low road. Get it out here, or describe when your ex acted like a petty bitch.

_____

_____

_____

_____

_____

_____

_____

_____

I DON'T MIND BEING ALONE. I JUST DO NOT WANT TO BE INSIGNIFICANT.

— Susie Myerson, The Marvelous Mrs. Maisel

I'm Right Here

Outside of your romantic relationships, what makes you feel significant? What makes you feel like you're leaving a mark?

_____

_____

_____

_____

_____

_____

_____

_____

_____

_____

_____

_____

OWNING UP
TO YOUR
VULNERABILITIES
IS A FORM OF
STRENGTH.

— Lizzo, NBC News

Stronger than Ever

None of that chin-up, stiff-upper-lip stuff. Your strength is in knowing what affects you the most and what boundaries should not be crossed.

What makes you feel most vulnerable inside or outside of a relationship?

_____

_____

_____

What about acknowledging your weaknesses could be helpful to you or to a partner?

_____

_____

_____

IF WE ONLY FELL IN LOVE
WITH PEOPLE WHO
WERE PERFECT FOR US...
THEN THERE WOULDN'T
BE SO MUCH FUSS
ABOUT LOVE IN
THE FIRST PLACE.

— Amor Towles, Rules of Civility

Better that Way

Some people get it "right" the first time. Others try again, and again, and again (and again!). There's a lot to be loved and learned from all those imperfect matches.

What about taking the long route has been beneficial for you?

_____

_____

_____

What would you have missed out on if you'd found "perfect" too early?

_____

_____

_____

LIFE BECOMES EASIER WHEN YOU LEARN TO ACCEPT AN APOLOGY YOU NEVER GOT.

— Robert Brault

In Lieu of Closure

Send yourself flowers. Not every relationship ends neatly, and the hardest ones to move past are those without resolutions or acknowledgment of hurt. What kind of apology would have helped? Imagine you had received this gift. How does it feel to release the burden of hoping someone will apologize?

_____

_____

_____

_____

_____

_____

_____

_____

WHEN I GET SAD, I STOP BEING SAD AND BE AWESOME INSTEAD.

— *Barney Stinson, How I Met Your Mother*

Way to Be!

Awesomeness doesn't just exit when sadness enters. What about you is awesome?

_____

_____

_____

_____

_____

_____

_____

_____

_____

_____

_____

_____

_____

I USED TO
THINK THAT
THE WORST THING
IN LIFE WAS TO
END UP ALL ALONE.
IT'S NOT.
THE WORST THING
IN LIFE IS ENDING UP
WITH PEOPLE WHO
MAKE YOU FEEL
ALL ALONE.

— *Lance Clayton, World's Greatest Dad*

Good People

Surround yourself with the people who make you feel like you're a part of something. Who does this for you? How do they make you feel loved?

_____

_____

_____

_____

_____

_____

_____

_____

_____

THE REASON
I TALK TO MYSELF
IS BECAUSE I'M
THE ONLY ONE
WHOSE ANSWERS
I ACCEPT.

— George Carlin

Take Your Own Advice

Ignoring the good, healthy, and well-intentioned advice
of all your loved ones and confidants sure is fun!

What's the best advice you can give to yourself?

_____

_____

_____

_____

What's the best advice you've received from someone else?

_____

_____

_____

_____

"LOVE MEANS
NEVER HAVING
TO SAY YOU'RE
SORRY."

— Erich Segal, Love Story

Never Apologize!

Okay, psycho. We've all heard the rom-com fallacies about what love is "actually." What bullshit notion about relationships have you had to unlearn?

_____

_____

_____

_____

_____

_____

_____

_____

MY ALONE
FEELS SO GOOD,
I'LL ONLY HAVE YOU
IF YOU'RE SWEETER
THAN MY SOLITUDE.

— Warsan Shire, Twitter

Bettersweet

Your solo emotional homeostasis is precious. If someone isn't making you feel as good or better than how you'd feel on your own, it's not the right relationship. What values should you look for in a partner that would only improve upon, rather than detract from, your life?

_____

_____

_____

_____

_____

_____

_____

_____

_____

_____

SPEND LESS
TIME TEARING
YOURSELF APART,
WORRYING IF YOU'RE
GOOD ENOUGH.
YOU ARE
GOOD ENOUGH.
AND YOU'RE GOING
TO MEET AMAZING
PEOPLE IN YOUR LIFE
WHO WILL HELP YOU
AND LOVE YOU.

— Reese Witherspoon, Glamour magazine

Don't Talk About My Friend That Way

If you wouldn't let your friend tear themselves down or be bullied, why would you do it to yourself?

What encouragement could you give yourself right now?

_____

_____

_____

Who should you have by your side?

_____

I'VE COME TO
THE CONCLUSION
THAT MY GUTS
HAVE SHIT
FOR BRAINS.

— Rob Gordon, High Fidelity

Listen to Your Gut (Maybe!)

Following your gut is super helpful if you have an internal compass. If you are someone who can't make sense of up or down in the paths of your relationships, joke's on you! Seek an alternate route.

Who or what makes a better compass?

_____

_____

What markers of a good relationship let you know you're on the right path?

_____

_____

_____

FUCK BEING A GOOD SPORT.

— Jennette McCurdy

All of This Is Optional!

Friendly reminder that you do not have to sit through the mansplaining session, the hobby you don't care about, or the thing that embarrasses you but you do anyway because the person you're dating likes it.

How can you shift your thinking so you don't feel forced into something that isn't for you?

_____

_____

_____

How would you rather be spending your time?

_____

_____

_____

YOU HAVE NOTHING TO PROVE TO ANYBODY.

— Maya Angelou

Exhibit A

When have you felt like you needed to prove your worth to a partner? What would you say to yourself now?

_____

_____

_____

_____

_____

_____

_____

_____

_____

_____

BEING SINGLE
USED TO MEAN
THAT NOBODY
WANTED YOU.
NOW IT MEANS
YOU'RE PRETTY SEXY
AND YOU'RE TAKING
YOUR TIME DECIDING
HOW YOU WANT
YOUR LIFE TO
BE AND WHO
YOU WANT TO
SPEND IT WITH.

— Carrie Bradshaw,
Sex and the City

What a Girl Wants

What feels most sexy and liberating about not being dependent upon a relationship? What could you do with your time?

_____

_____

_____

_____

_____

_____

_____

_____

_____

_____

_____

SUMMER BACHELORS LIKE SUMMER BREEZES, ARE NEVER AS COOL AS THEY PRETEND TO BE.

— Nora Ephron, New York Post

Real Cool, Bro

It's easy to make excuses for the ones who seem cool. Sure, he sleeps with his mattress on the floor because he's *an artist* and not because he's a man-child. He doesn't text back in a reasonable timeframe because he's just the busiest man on the planet. When did you wake up and realize your paramour was not all that cool?

_____

_____

_____

_____

_____

_____

_____

WE ALL FALL
FOR THE PRICK.
PRICKS ARE
SPONTANEOUS,
THEY'RE
UNPREDICTABLE,
AND THEY'RE FUN.
AND THEN WE'RE
SURPRISED WHEN
THEY TURN OUT
TO BE PRICKS.

— Alex Goran, Up in the Air

Bad Boys

When have you been attracted to someone who's bad news?
In what ways are you better off without their prickish presence?

_____

_____

_____

_____

_____

_____

_____

_____

_____

_____

_____

_____

WHY HAVEN'T I GOT A HUSBAND AND CHILDREN?

I NEVER MET A MAN I COULD MARRY.

— Greta Garbo

White Picket Fence

Watching everyone else hop, skip, and jump across those milestones can be a confusing experience. But not every milestone is right for everybody—in fact, it might just be annoying peer pressure buzzing in your ear. Bat those flies away. Which milestones aren't actually what you want?

_____

_____

_____

_____

_____

_____

_____

_____

A GIRL CAN WAIT
FOR THE RIGHT MAN
TO COME ALONG
BUT IN THE MEANTIME
THAT DOESN'T MEAN
SHE CAN'T HAVE A
WONDERFUL TIME WITH
ALL THE WRONG ONES.

— Cher

Mr. Right Now

"Flings are bad," blah blah blah, we get it. Not always. There's a difference between knowingly embarking on a bad situationship that will disappoint you and setting sail on the simple joy of a mutual respect for independence. What could a no-strings fling or serendipitous dalliance do for you?

_____

_____

_____

_____

_____

_____

_____

_____

_____

YOU WANNA FLY, YOU GOT TO GIVE UP THE SHIT THAT WEIGHS YOU DOWN.

— Toni Morrison, Song of Solomon

Time to Soar

Lighten your load here. What pressure, weight, or other burdens are you feeling that you need to release?

_____

_____

_____

_____

_____

_____

_____

_____

_____

_____

_____

RATHER THAN FOCUSING ON WHAT YOU LACK, FOCUS ON WHAT YOU HAVE: YOU.

— Natalie Lue

Endless Riches

You have more than you think you do. You're worth more than you account for. What qualities make you a great catch?

_____

_____

_____

_____

_____

_____

_____

_____

_____

_____

SOMETIMES YOU HAVE TO PUT UP A SIGN THAT SAYS "DO NOT DISTURB" ON YOUR HEART.

— Wiz Khalifa

Sorry, We're Closed

The open cracks of a broken heart are not gates of entry.
When you're recovering from a breakup or a romantic
disappointment, resist the urge to let someone else in before you're
ready. In what ways could you benefit from keeping out non-VIPs?

_____

_____

_____

_____

_____

_____

_____

_____

_____

WAS FEELIN' SO WEAK BUT BABY I'M STRONG. LITTLE DID I KNOW I'M A CHAMPION

— Bishop Briggs, "Champion"

Come Out Swinging

Not literally, because violence is bad. But you can train your heart to stand up for itself, to be resilient, to be a champion for your self-esteem.

In what ways do you feel strong?

_____

_____

_____

If you don't right now, what would your inner champion look like?

_____

_____

_____

I LOVE
BEING SINGLE.
IT'S ALMOST LIKE
BEING RICH.

— Sue Grafton

Life in Abundance

Calculate your emotional wealth. What do you have that makes you feel rich? What about life outside of a relationship could open doors?

_____

_____

_____

_____

_____

_____

_____

_____

_____

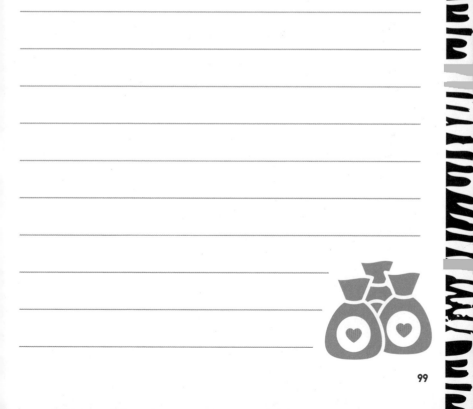

WANNA BE YOUR LOVER,

NOT YOUR FUCKING MOTHER.

— Katy Perry, "Circle the Drain"

Ugh, This Again

If you feel like you have emotionally spruced up every man you have ever dated and they find their forever person right after you—same girl, same. It still doesn't mean he was right for you. Don't stick around waiting for someone to mature. There are people out there who are ready for you. What do you want from a mature partner?

BE WARY OF MEN WITH SOMETHING TO PROVE.

— Taylor Jenkins Reid,
The Seven Husbands of Evelyn Hugo

You're So Vain

It's one thing to support a partner who is striving toward a goal. It's another to be in the splash zone of a narcissist with tunnel vision. What has this looked like for you?

_____

_____

_____

_____

_____

_____

_____

_____

_____

DON'T BE SCARED TO WALK ALONE.

DON'T BE SCARED TO LIKE IT.

— *John Mayer, "Age of Worry"*

Surprise, Surprise

You can find a whole lot of pretty in the world if you're not staring at the ground. What opportunities can you find in canceling a relationship that's bringing you down?

_____

_____

_____

_____

_____

_____

_____

_____

_____

_____

TO LOVE ONESELF IS THE BEGINNING OF A LIFELONG ROMANCE.

— Oscar Wilde, An Ideal Husband

Be Still
My Heart

Write a love letter to yourself. *(Seriously.)*

_____

_____

_____

_____

_____

_____

_____

_____

_____

_____

_____

WE NEED
TO LIVE
THE BEST
THAT'S
IN US.

— Angela Bassett

Show Up for Yourself

Not every day is a good day, and some low points last longer than others. But the best part of you is always there, tapping her fingernails waiting for you to be ready. When you're feeling like crap, what's one small gesture you can do for yourself so that best side shows up?

_____

_____

_____

_____

_____

_____

_____

_____

SOMEONE HAS TO STAND STILL FOR YOU TO LOVE THEM.

MY CHOICES ARE ALWAYS ON THE RUN.

— Carrie Fisher,
The Princess Diarist

Tag, You're It

Running is hard, and yet—inexplicably—people do it every day! Don't chase after someone who doesn't want you to follow, and don't play exhausting games when you could have more fun sitting still.

What scares you most about letting the runners get away?

_____

_____

_____

What could be waiting for you if you let them go?

_____

_____

_____

I'M SO FUCKIN' GRATEFUL FOR MY EX

THANK YOU, NEXT

— Ariana Grande, "thank u, next"

Good for Something

Exes come in all shapes and sizes. Some exes leave you with a sexy glow of a simple time gone by, and others sooner send you into a fit of rage than into a feeling of gratitude. What's one thing you can appreciate about a past romance? (Even if you need to end the sentence with "...because fuck that guy.")

_____

_____

_____

_____

_____

_____

_____

_____

TO FREE US FROM
THE EXPECTATIONS
OF OTHERS,
TO GIVE US
BACK TO OURSELVES—
THERE LIES THE GREAT,
SINGULAR POWER
OF SELF-RESPECT.

— Joan Didion, Vogue magazine

Put On
Your Cape

What do you value most about yourself? What about who you are as a person makes you most proud? Think about this as your superpower and wield it proudly.

_____

_____

_____

_____

_____

_____

_____

_____

_____

DISCOVER WHY
YOU'RE IMPORTANT,
THEN REFUSE
TO SETTLE
FOR ANYONE
WHO DOESN'T
COMPLETELY
AGREE.

— Fisher Amelie

Enthusiastic Consent

Yes, yes, yes! You are looking for the person who is as great as you are.

What makes you feel important?

_____

_____

_____

Why should you only entertain relationships with people who look at you and say, "Hell, Yes!"?

_____

_____

_____

SHE TOOK A STEP AND DIDN'T WANT TO TAKE ANY MORE, BUT SHE DID.

— *Markus Zusak, The Book Thief*

Keep It Moving, Sister

What's one small step forward on your personal journey?
Maybe it's deleting him from social media. Maybe it's taking up
pottery. Or maybe it's just giving yourself a little grace when you
need it. Describe how you'd take the first step and a few of the
ones to follow.

_____

_____

_____

_____

_____

_____

_____

_____

I AM MY OWN EXPERIMENT.

I AM MY OWN WORK OF ART.

— Madonna

Priceless
Artifact

Describe yourself in detail as if you were admiring a sculpture or a painting. What do you see?

_____

_____

_____

_____

_____

_____

_____

_____

_____

_____

DON'T SETTLE.

AS WITH ALL MATTERS OF THE HEART, YOU'LL KNOW WHEN YOU FIND IT.

— *Steve Jobs,*
Stanford Commencement

Ta-Da!

A lot of good can happen if you pay attention. Don't get distracted by things that don't feel right. How can you be more patient with yourself and the path in front of you? (Even if it feels like an endless, meandering schlep?)

_____

_____

_____

_____

_____

_____

_____

_____

_____

HE'S NOT
WORTH IT

Repeat it, scribble it, cross it out, or crinkle it up and burn it somewhere that will not cause a forest fire.

I AM
WORTH IT

Repeat it, color it, paste it on your wall for everyone to see.

Julie Day is a freelance writer and journalist living in Denver, Colorado. When she's not writing or traveling, she's hiking local trails with her two trusty spaniels, Todd and Copper.